HAL•LEONARD
INSTRUMENTAL
PLAY-ALONG

AUDIO ACCESS INCLUDED

PLAYBACK+
Speed • Pitch • Balance • Loop

CELLO

T0088855

Disney

ENCANTO

Audio arrangements by Peter Deneff

To access audio visit:
www.halleonard.com/mylibrary

Enter Code
5602-4737-7109-8373

ISBN 978-1-70516-363-4

HAL•LEONARD®

Visit Hal Leonard Online at
www.halleonard.com

Contact us:
Hal Leonard
7777 West Bluemound Road
Milwaukee, WI 53213
Email: info@halleonard.com

In Europe, contact:
Hal Leonard Europe Limited
42 Wigmore Street
Marylebone, London, W1U 2RN
Email: info@halleonardeurope.com

In Australia, contact:
Hal Leonard Australia Pty. Ltd.
4 Lentara Court
Cheltenham, Victoria, 3192 Australia
Email: info@halleonard.com.au

ALL OF YOU

CELLO

Music and Lyrics by
LIN-MANUEL MIRANDA

mp
p

COLOMBIA, MI ENCANTO

CELLO

Music and Lyrics by
LIN-MANUEL MIRANDA

THE FAMILY MADRIGAL

CELLO

Music and Lyrics by
LIN-MANUEL MIRANDA

DOS ORUGUITAS

CELLO

Music and Lyrics by
LIN-MANUEL MIRANDA

f

SURFACE PRESSURE

CELLO

Music and Lyrics by
LIN-MANUEL MIRANDA

mf
f
ff

WAITING ON A MIRACLE

CELLO

Music and Lyrics by
LIN-MANUEL MIRANDA

rit.

WE DON'T TALK ABOUT BRUNO

CELLO

Music and Lyrics by
LIN-MANUEL MIRANDA

mf
f

WHAT ELSE CAN I DO?

CELLO

Music and Lyrics by
LIN-MANUEL MIRANDA

To Coda
D.S. al Coda
CODA